BILLS PRE-GAMING

Tailgating as a Culinary Full-Contact Sport

Writing & Recipes by
Mark Donnelly, PhD.

Copyright © 2026 by Mark D. Donnelly, PhD.

Text, Photography, and Design by Mark D. Donnelly, PhD.

All rights reserved. No part of this publication may be reproduced, distributed, or transmitted in any form or by any means, including photocopying, recording, or other electronic or mechanical methods, without the prior written permission of the publisher, except in the case of brief quotations embodied in critical reviews and certain other non-commercial uses permitted by copyright law. For permission requests, write to the publisher at the address below.

RPSS - Rock Paper [Safety] Scissors Publishing
429 Englewood Avenue • Buffalo, New York 14223

www.rpsspublishing.com

Bills Pre-Game- Perfect Bound ISBN: 978-1-956688-67-2

Printed in the United States of America

17 18 19 20 21   6 5 4 3 2 1

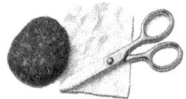

RPSS - Rock Paper [Safety] Scissors Publishing

DEDICATION:

For everyone who shows up early,
stays late,
and stand in the cold like it is part of the deal.

For the jackets that still smell like smoke and sauce.
For the parking spots that feel like home.

And for Buffalo,
where faith wears layers,
loyalty tastes like wings,
and next Sunday always starts now.

TABLE OF CONTENTS

Foreword
A Brief Explanation That Will - Not Actually Explain Anything - 7

Introduction
This Is Not a Party. This Is a Practice. -9

Chapter 1
Weather Is Just a Suggestion -11

Chapter 2
The Emotional Warm-Up -14

Chapter 3
Table Smashing as Celebration - 17

Chapter 4
Pinto Ron - 21

Chapter 5
Dress Code: Function First, Dignity Last -25

Chapter 6
Everyone is Seventeen

Chapter 7
Bills Mafia - 31

Chapter 8
The Throw That Comes Back -34

Chapter 8
Wings: Not a Recipe, a Moral Position -37

Chapter 9
Grilling in Hostile Conditions -45

Chapter 10
Chili, Stew, & Other Parking Lot Lifelines-5

Chapter 11
The Sacred Dip Table -61

Chapter 12
Classic Tailgate Game Changers -69

Chapter 13
Beer Is the Default Setting -79

Chapter 14
Shots, Thermoses, and Questionable Decisions -81

Chapter 15
The Grill You've Had Since Clinton Was President - 85

Chapter 16
The Sound System Arms Race -87

Chapter 17
The Regulars, the Newcomer, and the Keeper of Memory -90

Chapter 18
The Same Spot, Every Time -93

Chapter 19
Porta-Potties -95

Chapter 20
Flags and Moveable Art -98

Chapter 21
Lucky Gear and Unlucky Comments -102

Chapter 22
Victory Cleanup -103

Chapter 23
Loss Processing -104

Epilogue
Next Sunday Starts Now -106

BONUS SECTIONS
Tailgate Packing Checklist -108

A Short Glossary of Parking Lot Philosophy -112

About The Author -115

WHERE ELS[E] WOULD YOU RATHER BE?

Welcome to the Madness.
(An Explanation That Absolutely Won't Help)

Devoted N.F.L. fans show their love in ways that don't always survive being removed from context.

Green Bay Packers fans wear foam blocks of cheese on their heads, a decision that makes sense only if you've spent enough time in Wisconsin to stop asking follow-up questions. Raiders fans paint their faces in black and silver and spend the afternoon tormenting visiting players from a section called the Black Hole, which sounds less like seating and more like a warning. In Kansas City, Chiefs fans arrive in tricked-out school buses painted red and gold, proving that no one ever really outgrows the urge to personalize large vehicles.

Each of these traditions works. They look strange. They feel right. Context handles the rest.

Then there are Buffalo Bills fans.

Bills fans take the concept of devotion, remove the brakes, and see what happens. What looks ridiculous elsewhere becomes routine here through repetition, confidence, and a complete lack of concern for how it plays on television.

For years now, growing numbers of Bills tailgaters have concluded their pre- and postgame celebrations by climbing onto elevated objects – the back of a pickup truck, a retaining wall, occasionally the upper reaches of a Porta Potty – and launching themselves into folding tables below. The goal is simple: destroy the table, entertain friends, generate noise, and feel something before kickoff.

The tables never make it.

Phones come out. Cheers rise. Someone checks to make sure the jumper is vertical and smiling. Then food resumes.

Out of context, this behavior appears reckless.

In context, it's just how momentum is built.

And then there's Ken Pinto Ron Johnson.

If the folding table is the most visible symbol of Bills tailgating excess, Pinto Ron is its spiritual sibling. Where others leap downward, he looks upward, sees a goalpost, and decides condiments should travel farther than nature intended. Ketchup and mustard bottles take flight. Hot dogs follow. Nobody asks why. Everyone understands.

This is not vandalism.

This is ceremony.

Pinto Ron didn't invent Bills fandom, but he distilled something essential about it. That devotion doesn't need to be tidy. That joy can be loud, absurd, and communal. That sometimes the best way to say "we're still here" is to throw something bright into the air and let gravity finish the thought.

This book is not here to explain how to jump through tables or launch condiments responsibly. It's here to explain how a fan base arrives at a place where these things make sense at all. How weather, history, heartbreak, and stubborn loyalty combine into rituals that look unhinged until you understand what they're holding together.

Buffalo tailgating isn't about stunts. The table is just wood and hinges. The condiments are just sauce. The real act is showing up early, feeding strangers, standing shoulder to shoulder in conditions that discourage it, and doing it again next week no matter how the last one ended.

If you're from Buffalo, none of this needs defending.

If you're not, consider this fair warning.

Context is coming.

The grill is lit.

The table is folding.

And somewhere, ketchup is already in the air.

INTRODUCTION
This Is Not a Party. This Is a Practice.

Somewhere along the way, someone decided to call this "tailgating."

That word is doing far too little work.

A party implies options. You can arrive late. You can leave early. You can pretend you're just stopping by. Buffalo tailgating does not recognize any of these concepts. Once you cross the parking lot threshold, time behaves differently. Weather becomes a rumor. Hunger becomes a strategy problem.

This is not a social gathering. It is a weekly rehearsal in loyalty, logistics, and light defiance.

If you're looking for folding tables in their original condition, you're already lost.

Buffalo tailgating operates on an internal logic that makes perfect sense once you stop asking why. Grills appear in conditions that suggest legal intervention. Coolers are packed with the confidence of people who have done this before and plan to do it again. Food is shared immediately, without paperwork or background checks. If you hesitate, someone will hand you a plate anyway.

You'll notice the absence of small talk. No one asks what you do for a living. They ask what you're cooking, where you parked, and whether you've ever tried that sauce before. These are not casual questions. They determine trust.

There is also a sound to Buffalo tailgating. It's not just music, though music helps. It's the rhythm of lids slamming shut, burners igniting, cans opening in sequence. It's laughter that carries farther in cold air. It's the unmistakable voice of someone retelling a play that happened years ago as if it just ended ten minutes ago and still needs to be discussed.

This culture did not appear overnight. It was built season by season, disappointment by disappointment, Sunday by Sunday. You don't tailgate like this unless you've decided, consciously or not, that showing up matters more than outcomes.

That decision changes everything.

It changes how you pack.

It changes how you dress.

It changes how you define success before the first snap.

Winning is wonderful. Losing is familiar. Tailgating is constant.

This book is not here to teach you how to behave sensibly. It will not tell you how to stay clean, dry, or emotionally neutral. It will, however, explain why nobody here expects those things in the first place.

Think of this as a field guide. A translation manual. A slightly unhinged love letter to parking lots that briefly become neighborhoods and strangers who become allies by noon.

If you already do this, you'll recognize yourself on these pages.

If you don't, read carefully. You're being invited in.

The grill is warming up.

Someone is yelling directions that no one follows.

Kickoff is closer than it feels.

Let's begin.

CHAPTER ONE
Weather Is Just a Suggestion

The forecast is lying to you.

Not because meteorologists are bad at their jobs, but because Buffalo tailgating exists outside their jurisdiction. Snow totals, wind advisories, and phrases like "feels like" are useful for errands. They are largely decorative on game day.

In Buffalo, weather is not a condition. It is a character. An unreliable one. Loud. Occasionally aggressive. Always present. And absolutely not in charge.

Elsewhere, cold cancels plans. Here, it sharpens them.

The first rule of Buffalo tailgating is this: if the game is happening, so is the grill. Rain, sleet, lake-effect snow, sideways ice needles that feel personal—none of it counts as a reason. At most, it's a note. Something you acknowledge while tightening your hood and checking the propane.

You will see grills operating in conditions that suggest a dare. Flames fighting wind like they have something to prove. Smoke blowing directly into the face of the person cooking, who will not move. This is not stubbornness. This is form.

Cold air changes everything. Sound travels farther. Smells linger longer. Hunger arrives early and refuses to leave. Food matters more when your hands are numb. Hot things are not a preference; they are a survival strategy.

This is why chili shows up before noon. Why soup is served from thermoses built for construction sites. Why someone always has a backup plan involving melted cheese and bread.

The clothing situation reflects the same philosophy. Layers are added without apology and without symmetry. Parkas over jerseys. Snow pants with face paint. Gloves removed briefly for tasks requiring dexterity, then replaced immediately, like pit stops in a race no one admits they're running.

Fashion is not dead here. It's just pragmatic.

Every newcomer asks the same question:

"Aren't you cold?"

This is the wrong question.

The correct question is: "Are you prepared?"

Prepared people bring hand warmers. Prepared people know which cooler holds the drinks and which one holds the food that must not freeze. Prepared people understand that beer left on the ground is now beer-flavored ice and plan accordingly.

Prepared people also know when to stop talking about the weather entirely.

At a certain point, complaining becomes inefficient. The cold isn't listening. The wind has already made its decision. The snow does not care how long you've been a fan.

So the conversation shifts. Toward food. Toward stories. Toward who parked where and how early they got there. Toward the one game that still bothers everyone for reasons no one needs to explain.

Weather fades into the background. It becomes the frame, not the subject.

And here's the part outsiders miss: none of this feels heroic while it's happening. It feels normal. Familiar. Reassuring, even. There is comfort in doing the same unreasonable thing at the same time every week with people who understand why you're doing it.

The weather will do whatever it wants.

The team will do whatever it does.

The grill will be lit.

That's not optimism.

That's the system working as designed.

By the time kickoff arrives, your face is numb, your hands are warm, and you're standing exactly where you planned to be.

The forecast never stood a chance.

CHAPTER TWO
The Emotional Warm-Up

Nobody shows up to a Buffalo tailgate emotionally cold.

That would be dangerous.

This fan base does not stroll into game day casually, like people expecting a light jog. We arrive pre-loaded. Decades of memory, near-misses, miracles, collapses, comebacks, and games that still come up uninvited in conversation have already stretched the emotional muscles long before the first burner clicks on.

Tailgating is how we finish the warm-up.

Some cities ease into optimism. Buffalo treats it like a contact sport. You don't just feel good about a game. You negotiate with yourself. You acknowledge the past. You make a quiet promise not to get carried away, then immediately violate it by the time the grill lid closes.

The parking lot is where this emotional calibration happens.

You'll hear it in the conversations. They begin carefully.

"How you feeling about today?"

"Looks good on paper."

"We'll see."

These are not throwaway lines. They are protective equipment.

Every fan here has learned, through repetition, that hope needs supervision. Too much too early and it pulls something. So we stretch it gently. We reference injuries. We mention matchups. We remind ourselves of weather, officiating, and the unpredictable nature of football itself.

Then someone brings up a past game. Not the worst one. Not yet. Just enough to keep everyone honest.

This is not pessimism. It's muscle memory.

Food plays a critical role in the process. Eating together creates balance. Wings steady the nerves. Chili slows down runaway predictions. Dips keep hands busy so people don't gesture wildly while explaining exactly how this game could go sideways.

You'll notice that optimism tends to peak somewhere between the second plate and the first beer. This is the sweet spot. Confidence feels earned. Hope feels reasonable. Someone says, "If we play our game," and nobody argues because that sentence has already done its job.

Music helps too. The playlist is never accidental. It contains songs that have survived multiple eras. Tracks that remind people who they were when they first started caring this much. The volume rises, not to hype, but to blur the edge of overthinking.

Laughter shows up early. Loud, unfiltered, and often at someone's expense. Humor is a pressure valve. If you can joke about it, you can carry it.

By the time kickoff approaches, something shifts. The analysis slows. The stories repeat. Plates are lighter. The emotional muscles are loose, warmed, and ready for impact.

This is when you'll see the quiet moments.

Someone staring at the stadium.

Someone adjusting the same hat they always wear.

Someone saying nothing at all.

They're not nervous. They're focused.

Buffalo fans don't need pep talks. We don't need reminders to care. We need a few hours together to remember how to care without tearing something important.

The tailgate does that work.

By the time you pack up and start walking in, you're not just fed. You're centered. Calibrated. Properly braced for whatever comes next.

The emotional warm-up is complete.

Now it's time to play.

CHAPTER THREE
Table Smashing as Celebration

At some point, Buffalo looked at a folding table and decided it was asking for too much respect.

Elsewhere, tables are for holding things. Plates. Cups. Conversations. In Buffalo tailgating culture, the folding table evolved. It became symbolic. Temporary. Aspirational. Something that knew, deep down, it was never meant to survive the afternoon.

Table smashing did not begin as spectacle. It began as release.

A surplus of energy. A surplus of emotion. A moment where cheering was no longer sufficient and gravity felt like it wanted to be involved.

The first table to break probably surprised everyone. The second one made it feel intentional. By the third, the crowd understood what was happening and adjusted accordingly.

This is not vandalism.

This is punctuation.

The mechanics are simple. Elevation is found. A pickup truck tailgate. A retaining wall. Something sturdy enough to launch from but not sturdy enough to invite reconsideration. A folding table is positioned below, never new, never expensive, always pre-accepted as a loss.

Someone climbs. The crowd forms instinctively. Phones rise. Encouragement becomes loud and strangely supportive. Safety checks happen without ceremony. "You good?" is asked. "Yeah," is confirmed.

Then gravity takes over.

The table collapses exactly as designed. Hinges surrender. Legs fold inward. The sound is unmistakable. The jumper stands, arms raised, still intact. Cheers erupt. High-fives follow. The remains are moved aside respectfully.

Table smashing is not about destruction. It's about transformation. A folding table begins the day as furniture and ends it as proof that joy exceeded containment. That the moment demanded something louder than words.

It is also, quietly, about trust.

The jumper trusts the crowd. The crowd trusts the jumper. Everyone trusts the table to fail in a predictable way. This shared understanding is what keeps it from becoming reckless. There is chaos here, but it is informed chaos.

Newcomers react the same way every time. Shock first. Laughter second. Then curiosity. Then, occasionally, planning.

Veterans know when it's coming. There's a rhythm to it. It doesn't happen randomly. It arrives at emotional peaks. After a big win. Before a big game. When the energy tips from contained to collective.

And when it's over, the tailgate resumes immediately.

Table smashing is not required. Many people never do it. Many never want to. But its presence in the culture serves a purpose. It reminds everyone that this thing we care about is supposed to be felt, not managed.

It's not about pain.

It's not about bravado.

It's about release.

The folding table is chosen precisely because it breaks easily. It absorbs impact so people don't have to. It gives the moment somewhere to go.

And when the day winds down, when the lot empties and the grills cool, the broken table remains as evidence.

Not of recklessness.

Of enthusiasm exceeding capacity.

Which, in Buffalo, feels about right.

CHAPTER FOUR
Pinto Ron

Every great Buffalo tradition eventually stops being folklore and starts being history.

Ken Pinto Ron Johnson was born in 1957, which matters only because it means he has outlasted trends, coaching eras, playoff droughts, and several ideas that would have sent other people home early. Better known simply as Pinto Ron, Johnson is one of the rare figures in sports fandom whose legend is not exaggerated. If anything, it's underreported.

From 1994 through 2020, Pinto Ron attended every single Buffalo Bills game, home and away. Not most. Not almost. Every one. That includes snowstorms, losing seasons, and the 2015 Bills–Jaguars game in London, which required crossing an ocean just to remain consistent.

Consistency matters here.

By profession, Johnson is a software engineer. This explains a great deal. Precision. Problem-solving. The ability to look at a system and say, "Yes, this can be pushed further." By passion, he is a tailgate architect whose primary building material just happened to be a red Ford Pinto.

The Ford Pinto

The car is not a prop. It is infrastructure.

An aging red Ford Pinto became the nucleus of what would evolve into one of the most recognizable tailgates in the NFL. Over decades, the Pinto stopped being transportation and became a fixed point in Buffalo game-day geography. Fans didn't ask where the party was. They asked if the Pinto was there.

It always was.

Extreme Cooking, Properly Explained

Pinto Ron's cooking methods look unhinged until you understand the logic: heat is heat, surface is surface, and commitment is the missing ingredient.

Food was cooked directly on the hood of the Pinto using objects never intended to appear in a kitchen. Shovels. Army helmets. Saw blades. Filing cabinets. Toolboxes. Oil pans. If it could hold heat and not immediately fail, it was promoted to cookware.

This wasn't recklessness. It was applied confidence.

Bacon sizzled. Wings cooked evenly. Pizza came out of a metal filing cabinet oven. Omelets landed on shovel blades at dawn. Pulled pork smoked in a Buick oil pan. The food wasn't a joke. It was good. That mattered.

The Condiments and the Bowling Ball

Then there were the traditions.

One of the most recognizable rituals at the Red Pinto Tailgate was Johnson being ceremonially doused in ketchup and mustard. Not splashed. Not dabbed. Fully coated. This wasn't humiliation. It was gratitude. A visual expression of devotion that Buffalo understands instinctively.

And then there was the bowling ball.

For years, Pinto Ron served shots of cherry liqueur from a 16-pound bowling ball, poured through the thumbhole in a ritual that combined precision, trust, and questionable judgment. It became so iconic that the National Football League eventually stepped in and shut it down.

Briefly.

Johnson responded the only way Buffalo responds to overreach: by moving the tailgate to private property next to the stadium, where the NFL had no jurisdiction. The bowling ball returned. Order was restored.

Why He Matters

Pinto Ron isn't famous because he's loud. He's famous because he never left.

Through snow, sleet, losing streaks, and playoff droughts, the Red Pinto Tailgate never missed a game. What began as a few friends horsing around became an institution. Part sideshow. Part soup kitchen. Entirely sincere.

Fans, strangers, rivals, and first-timers were welcomed without question. Stories were shared. Food was handed out. Loyalty was practiced publicly, not explained privately.

Johnson has been featured in multiple NFL Films productions, not because he sought attention, but because the story kept insisting on being told.

The Legacy

Pinto Ron represents something rare in sports culture: endurance without bitterness, absurdity without irony, and joy without conditions.

He didn't build a brand.

He kept a promise.

That no matter the weather, the record, or the year, Buffalo fans would have a place to gather, eat, laugh, and remember why they came.

You don't recreate the Red Pinto Tailgate.

You document it.

Because once something lasts long enough, it stops being chaos.

It becomes tradition.

CHAPTER FIVE
Dress Code: Function First, Dignity Last

Buffalo tailgating has a dress code.

It is not written down.

It is not enforced.

It is absolutely followed.

The rule is simple: wear whatever allows you to stay outside longer than common sense would recommend. Everything else is optional, negotiable, or proudly abandoned.

This is why you will see combinations that defy logic, fashion, and meteorology. Jerseys layered over hoodies layered under parkas. Snow pants paired with sneakers that should have retired during a previous administration. A balaclava topped with a novelty hat shaped like an animal that does not live in this climate.

From a distance, it looks chaotic. Up close, it's applied science.

Every garment has a purpose. Jerseys declare allegiance. Coats trap heat. Scarves function as insulation, face protection, or celebratory props. Gloves come in two categories: the warm ones and the ones you can still open a beer in. The truly experienced bring both.

Then there are Zubaz.

Zubaz is not clothing. It is a statement that says, "I understand where I am, and I am not afraid of it."

The bold stripes. The aggressive patterns. The complete rejection of subtlety. Zubaz exists because Buffalo decided that if you're already cold, you might as well be loud about it. These pants offer minimal insulation, maximum visibility, and an unmistakable confidence that suggests the wearer has been doing this for a long time.

Zubaz pairs well with everything because it pairs well with nothing. Jerseys, hoodies, snow boots, sneakers, face paint, no face paint, optimism, regret, all of it works. Once Zubaz enters the outfit, coherence becomes irrelevant.

Footwear remains a practical affair. Tailgaters traverse parking lots that alternate between ice, slush, and mystery puddles. Waterproof beats new. Traction beats pride. Anyone wearing clean shoes is either visiting or about to learn something important.

Face paint continues to defy reason. Cold locks it in. Wind weathers it. Snow adds texture. By kickoff, many fans resemble abstract art pieces titled Commitment.

Hats tell stories. The older the hat, the more credibility it carries. Faded logos indicate experience. Stains are not flaws; they are footnotes. When someone says, "I've had this since the Flutie years," the conversation ends respectfully.

Costumes exist outside all known rules. They are not required, but they are supported. If someone shows up wearing something wildly impractical, the group compensates. Extra layers are offered. Heat sources are adjusted. This is how Buffalo takes care of its own.

The question outsiders always ask is, "Aren't you worried how you look?"

This misunderstands the assignment.

Buffalo tailgating is not about looking good. It's about lasting long enough to tell the story afterward. By the end, dignity has been traded for warmth, mobility, and the quiet satisfaction of knowing you dressed correctly for the conditions you refused to avoid.

And if you didn't?

Zubaz probably would have helped.

CHAPTER SIX
Everyone is Seventeen

At some point during a Buffalo tailgate, you look around and realize something unsettling.

Everyone is you.

Not literally, but numerically. The parking lot has become a sea of 17s. Jerseys layered over hoodies. Hoodies layered under parkas. Seventeen stitched, screened, embroidered, vintage, knockoff, limited edition, signed, unsigned, and questionably washed.

You are not sure when this happened. You just know it did.

There are other numbers, technically. A few brave souls still rock throwbacks. Someone's wearing something ironic from a darker era. But those jerseys behave like dialects. Seventeen is the language.

This is not bandwagon behavior. Buffalo does not do bandwagons. This is alignment.

Josh Allen did not just become a quarterback. He became a shared decision. A citywide nod that says, "Yes. This. We're going with this."

The jersey shows up early. You see it before coffee. Before the grill lights. Before the weather has fully introduced itself. It's worn with confidence and zero explanation. No one asks why you're wearing it. Asking would imply doubt.

The variations tell stories.

There's the pristine one that only comes out for home games and important conversations. There's the faded one that has seen things. There's the oversized one worn over four layers because warmth matters more than silhouette. There's the youth-sized one stretched heroically over adulthood.

Some jerseys are customized. Some are clearly older than the haircut being worn beneath them. Some still have tags tucked discreetly inside because superstition is complicated.

Wearing 17 is not a statement you make out loud. It's a condition you enter. It says you're opting into the collective mood. That you're ready to feel hopeful without pretending you haven't been hurt before.

Children wear 17 like prophecy. Adults wear it like permission. Older fans wear it carefully, as if not to spook anything.

And yes, there are debates. About stats. About decisions. About moments that should have gone differently. These debates happen within the jersey, not against it. The number does not require perfection. It requires effort, resilience, and the occasional impossible throw that makes everyone forget what they were worried about.

Late in the tailgate, after the food has settled and the music has peaked, you'll see it clearly. A group photo forms accidentally. Arms around shoulders. Breath visible in the air.

All 17s.

Different sizes. Different conditions. Same number.

It's not uniformity. It's agreement.

Agreement that this is the moment you're in.

Agreement that you're here together.

Agreement that hope, this time, feels earned.

When the walk to the stadium begins, the jerseys move as a unit. Seventeen flowing forward, steady and loud enough to feel like momentum.

And if you're not wearing one?

That's fine.

Someone nearby has an extra.

CHAPTER SEVEN
Bills Mafia

(The loud part you see, and the quiet part that pays the bills.)

Bills Mafia did not start as branding.

That's the first thing to understand.

It started as recognition.

Someone noticed that what was happening in Buffalo didn't look like normal fandom. It was louder. Wetter. More committed. And strangely generous. So someone named it, half-joking, fully accurate, and the name stuck because there was no better one.

Bills Mafia isn't an organization. It's a condition.

But like all conditions, it has catalysts.

One of them is Del Reid.

Reid didn't invent Bills fans. He helped give them a mirror. In 2011, he helped ignite the #BillsMafia hashtag on Twitter, accidentally turning scattered, passionate fans into something visible, connected, and powerful.

What followed wasn't just louder cheering.

It was coordination.

And then came the money.

Not for parties.

For people.

Del Reid is also the founder of 26 Shirts, a charitable apparel company that turned sports fandom into a reliable engine for community good. Shirts went up. Funds rolled in. Families were helped. Causes were supported. Buffalo showed, repeatedly, that it could be ridiculous and responsible in the same breath.

That duality matters.

Bills Mafia is known nationally for broken tables, flying condiments, and clips that make morning shows squint nervously. But what often follows those clips is a donation link. A fundraiser. A quietly staggering total raised in a very short amount of time.

Break a table.

Then rebuild something.

That's the rhythm.

This is why Bills Mafia confuses people. It doesn't fit the stereotype. It's rowdy, yes. But it's also deeply civic. The same fans who jump off pickup trucks will empty their wallets for hospitals, charities, players' foundations, and strangers who suddenly need help.

It's chaos with a conscience.

The Mafia has its icons.

Superfans like Bills Elvis (John Lang, *left*), and his outrageous guitars who proves that rhinestones and cold weather can coexist. Personalities who show up so consistently they become landmarks. You don't ask if they'll be there. You just look for them.

And then there are the celebrity members. People who found Buffalo fandom accidentally and never left. Christopher McDonald,

Wolf Blitzer, Anderson Cooper, Luke Russert. They don't dilute the culture. They validate it. Proof that once you see this thing up close, it's hard not to respect it.

Del Reid's role in all this was never about attention. It was about direction. He helped turn a fan base's raw energy into a philanthropic force without sanding down its edges. That balance earned him the 2023 Bills Fan of the Year award, which felt less like an individual honor and more like a thank-you note handed to the entire parking lot.

Because Bills Mafia isn't about leaders telling people what to do.

It's about someone saying, "We could help," and thousands of people replying, "Yeah. Obviously."

That's the part outsiders miss.

Bills Mafia is not reckless devotion. It's family.

It's practiced loyalty.

It understands that caring deeply about something means occasionally looking ridiculous and frequently being useful. It knows joy is louder when it's shared, and grief is lighter when it's distributed.

You don't have to break a table.

You don't have to wear a costume.

You don't even have to be on social media.

You just have to show up when it counts.

That's the Mafia.

Loud when necessary.

Generous by default.

And always, somehow, still here.

Photo by: Emily Donnelly

CHAPTER EIGHT
The Throw That Comes Back

Every Buffalo tailgate has a football.-

Not the game ball. Not anything official. A scuffed one. A faded one. Sometimes one with tape holding the seams together out of stubbornness more than necessity. It lives in the trunk until it doesn't. At some point, without announcement, it's out.

And when it does, the parking lot opens up just enough for the truth to be revealed.

Playing catch at a Buffalo tailgate is not a game. It's an evaluation.

This is where fathers teach sons things they cannot put into sentences. Grip. Spin. Eye contact. How to move your feet without announcing that you're thinking about moving your feet. It's a rite of passage disguised as something casual.

"Just toss it," Dad says, already knowing whether you're about to confirm or disappoint him.

The throw tells the story immediately.

There's the clean spiral. No wobble. No apology. The ball arrives chest-high, soft enough to catch, firm enough to respect. This throw belongs to someone who played football. Maybe not professionally. Maybe not well. But enough to know what the ball wants to do if you don't get in its way.

The first time a ball comes in hot and they don't flinch, something changes. The first clean catch echoes louder than the grill lid. Pride is registered. It's subtle, but it's there.

Around them, the parking lot provides commentary.

"Nice spiral."

"You played, didn't you?"

"Back up, give 'em room."

Other dads wander over, drawn by the sound of leather hitting palms. Uncles join. Cousins. Someone's buddy who insists he "used to play quarterback" until his first throw reveals otherwise.

Nobody laughs. Nobody needs to.

The football is democratic but unforgiving.

The distance increases naturally. Ten yards. Then more. Jackets come off. Beer is placed carefully on bumpers. A son overthrows a little. A father adjusts his route without mentioning it. That's teaching.

Eventually, the football becomes communal. Three-person drills form accidentally. A stranger asks to jump in and is accepted based solely on how he throws the ball back. No résumé required.

And always, somewhere nearby, there's that guy.

The one who claps loudly.

Who yells "I'm open!" while standing five feet away.

Who catches the ball against his chest like it's a live animal.

He's that kid who wore black socks in gym class.

Late in the tailgate, the throws slow down. The ball comes back in shorter arcs. The father hands it to the son and says, "One more," even though both know it won't be the last one ever.

The ball is tucked away. The lesson is complete.

Years later, the son will bring his own kid. The ball will come out again. The parking lot will open. The legacy will resume.

It's tradition.

CHAPTER NINE
Wings: Not a Recipe, a Moral Position

In Buffalo, wings are not food.

They are a declaration.

You can tell a lot about a person by how they approach wings. How they order them. How they talk about them. How quiet they get when the topic turns serious. This is not snobbery. It's quality control.

At a Buffalo tailgate, wings are the anchor. Everything else is negotiable. Chili can vary. Burgers can improvise. Dips can experiment dangerously close to heresy. Wings do not wander.

They arrive hot.

They arrive unapologetic.

They arrive without ranch.

If you brought ranch, that's fine. It can stay closed. For now.

Buffalo wings are about balance. Heat and tang. Fat and acid. Crunch and surrender. They are not drowned. They are coated. They are not stacked delicately. They are piled with confidence.

And they are shared immediately. Nobody waits. Nobody plates carefully. You take one, then another, then you start explaining why these are "done right," even if no one asked.

Below are six tailgate-tested wing recipes. They are written plainly because wings do not need poetry. They need heat, timing, and respect.

Old School Chicken Wings

Instructions

In a heavy-bottomed Dutch oven or electric deep fryer heat oil to 375°F.

Prepare the wings by cutting them into three sections and discarding the tip. Pat them dry.

In a medium sauce pot set over low heat, melt butter and add hot sauce and stir until fully incorporated.

Fry wings in small batches until crispy on the outside and no longer pink on the inside. Drain on paper towels. Transfer wings to a large bowl containing sauce and carefully toss to coat.

Serve with celery sticks and blue cheese dressing … and an old growth forest worth of napkins.

Ingredients

Oil for frying

5 lbs. Chicken wings

8 tablespoons (1 stick) butter

5 tablespoons Frank's hot sauce

(Optional: Garlic and Onion Powder)

Celery sticks

Blue cheese dressing

Garlic Parmesan Wings

Ingredients

3 lbs. Chicken wings

Salt and pepper

Sauce

1/2 cup melted butter

4 cloves garlic, minced

1/2 cup grated Parmesan cheese

1 tablespoon chopped parsley

Black pepper to taste

Instructions

In a heavy-bottomed Dutch oven or electric deep fryer heat oil to 375°F.

Prepare the wings by cutting them into three sections and discarding the tip. Pat them dry.

Cook wings until crispy.

Warm butter and garlic together just until fragrant.

Toss wings in butter-garlic mixture.

Sprinkle with Parmesan and parsley.

Tailgate Law:

These are not "Buffalo wings," but they are allowed near them

Flamin' Hot Cheetos Wings

Instructions

Preheat oven to 425°F.

Prepare the wings by cutting them into three sections and discarding the tip. Pat them dry.

Season chicken wings with salt and pepper, then dredge in flour. Next, dip wings in egg, and then in Cheetos crumbs.

Arrange chicken in an even layer on a large baking sheet and bake for 18 to 20 minutes, or until chicken is cooked through.

In a small bowl combine hot sauce, honey, and butter. Microwave, whisking every 15 seconds until butter is melted and mixture is combined.

Pour hot sauce mixture over wings and arrange on platter.

Ingredients

2 lbs. Chicken wings

Kosher salt

Freshly ground black pepper

1/3 cup all-purpose flour

2 large eggs, beaten

1 (8.5-oz.) bag Flamin' Hot Cheetos, crushed

1/4 cup Frank's hot sauce

2 tablespoons honey

4 tablespoons butter

Grilled Wings

Ingredients

2 lbs. Chicken wings

Vegetable oil, for grill

Frank's hot sauce or BBQ sauce

Instructions

Prepare the wings by cutting them into three sections and discarding the tip. Pat them dry.

Grill wings over indirect heat until nearly done. Move to direct flame briefly to char.

Toss with classic hot sauce or BBQ sauce.

Return to grill for 1–2 minutes to set sauce.

Remove before regret.

Tailgate Law:

Char is flavor. Burn is a mistake.

Know the difference.

Guinness Wings

Instructions

Prep wings by cutting them into three sections and discarding the tip. Pat them dry.

Combine everything except for Guinness in a large bowl and mix well. Leave to marinate about 15 minutes. Drain off marinade and reserve.

Heat 4 tbs oil in a wok or deep pan till smoking hot. Add chicken and stir over high heat till browned. Pour in reserved marinade and continue stirring till sticky. Keep heat high.

Pour in Guinness and bring to the boil. Lower heat and simmer till liquid evaporates and chicken is cooked through and coated with thick and sticky gravy, but not falling off bones. Stir, scraping bottom and sides often to prevent sticking and scorching.

Ingredients

5 lbs. Chicken wings

10 shallots, peeled and chopped

2 teaspoons black pepper

1/2 cup soy sauce

4 teaspoons sugar

1/4 cup oil

2 bottles Guinness stout
  (1 bottle for recipe,
   1 bottle for enjoying while cooking)

Loganberry Wings

Ingredients

1-1/2 cups Loganberry jam

1/3 cup Balsamic vinegar

3 tablespoons soy sauce

1-1/2 teaspoons crushed red pepper

5 lbs. Chicken wings

Instructions

Preheat the oven to 400°F. Line two baking sheets with aluminum foil.

In a small saucepan, combine the Loganberry jam, Balsamic vinegar, soy sauce, and crushed red pepper over medium heat, stirring until smooth.

Prep wings by cutting them into three sections and discarding the tip. Pat them dry.

In a large bowl, toss the wings with half of the jam mixture.

Place on the baking sheets and bake for 50 minutes.

Turn the wings and brush with the remaining jam mixture.

Bake for 8 to 10 more minutes, or until no pink remains in the chicken and the sauce glazes the wings.

CHAPTER TEN
Grilling in Hostile Conditions

At some point during every Buffalo tailgate, someone will say, "This grill's acting up."

This is not a complaint.

It is an observation, delivered calmly, while snow blows sideways and the flame behaves like it has a personality disorder.

Grilling in Buffalo is not about ideal conditions. It's about adaptability, patience, and knowing when to stop fiddling with the knobs and just let it ride. Lids freeze shut. Wind steals heat. Gloves make fine motor skills theoretical. None of this stops the process.

The grill is still the center of gravity. People orbit it. Conversations happen near it. Hands drift toward it for warmth and purpose. Whoever is tending it gains temporary authority, regardless of whether they asked for it.

What follows are six grill recipes designed specifically for parking lots, cold fingers, uneven heat, and the understanding that perfection is less important than momentum.

These are forgiving recipes. They survive wind gusts. They tolerate distractions. They reward confidence.

Classic Burgers

Instructions

Form patties slightly larger than the buns. Do not overwork.

Season both sides generously with salt and pepper.

Grill over medium-high heat, lid down when possible.

Flip once, add cheese if using.

Serve immediately.

Tailgate Law:

If someone suggests stuffing the burgers, hand them a drink and keep grilling.

Ingredients

2 lbs ground beef (80/20)

1½ teaspoon kosher salt

1 teaspoon black pepper

6 burger buns

Optional toppings:

American cheese, onions, pickles

Grilled Sausage with Peppers & Onions

Ingredients

1 large Vidalia onion cut into thin strips

2 tablespoons olive oil

16 oz jarred roasted red peppers

Salt and pepper to taste

6 Italian sausage

6 sausage buns

Instructions

Preheat your grill to medium heat.

In a cast iron pan saute the onions and peppers in olive oil. Toss with salt and pepper.

Remove from grill very carefully (remember that pan is

Grill Italian Sausage until fully cooked.

Place in buns and serve with peppers and onions.

Hot Dogs

Ingredients

All-beef hot dogs -As many as you have

Buns

Optional toppings: mustard, onions, relish

Serves: Hungry hordes

Instructions

Grill dogs slowly, rolling often.

Look for blistered skins, not blackened regret.

Warm buns briefly.

Serve without commentary.

Tailgate Law: Hot dogs feed everyone while the real food finishes.

Chicken Thighs

Instructions

In a small bowl, mix the olive oil, Dijon mustard, lemon juice, Worcestershire sauce, garlic powder, onion powder, dried thyme and kosher salt.

Pat the chicken thighs dry with a paper towel. Add the chicken to a container and pour on the marinade. Use your hands to evenly cover the chicken with the marinade. Marinate in the refrigerator for at least 30 minutes.

Preheat a grill to medium-high heat (375°F to 450°F).

Grill the chicken thighs smooth side down until you see grill marks and it releases from the grates, 5 to 6 minutes for small thighs and 6 to 8 for large thighs. Flip and cook until the internal temperature is 165°F, 4 to 5 minutes.

Remove and rest for 5 minutes.

Ingredients

8 large or 12 small chicken thighs, boneless skinless or bone-in, skin-on (about 3 pounds)

2 tablespoons olive oil

1 tablespoon Dijon mustard

1 tablespoon lemon juice

1 teaspoon Worcestershire sauce or A1 sauce

1 teaspoon smoked paprika

1 teaspoon garlic powder

1 teaspoon onion powder

¼ teaspoon dried thyme

2 teaspoons kosher salt

Grilled Shrimp

Instructions

Soak wooden skewers in water for 30 minutes.

In a large bowl, whisk garlic, oil, lime juice, honey, soy sauce, and Sriracha. Reserve 1/4 cup marinade. Add shrimp to remaining marinade and toss to combine.

Prepare a grill for medium-high heat; heat 5 minutes (or heat a grill pan over medium-high heat). Thread shrimp onto skewers.

Grill shrimp, occasionally turning and brushing with marinade, until pink and opaque, (about 3 minutes per side).

Ingredients

4 garlic cloves, minced

1/4 cup extra-virgin olive oil

1/4 cup lime juice

3 tablespoons honey

2 tablespoons soy sauce

1 tablespoon Sriracha

2 lbs. shrimp, peeled, deveined

Lime wedges, for serving

Chicken on the Throne (Beer Can Chicken)

Ingredients

1 (4-pound) whole chicken

2 tablespoons extra virgin olive oil or other vegetable oil

1 (12-ounce) can beer, room temperature, opened and half-full

1 tablespoon kosher salt or sea salt

2 tablespoons chopped fresh thyme leaves, or 1 tablespoon dried thyme

1 tablespoon black pepper

Instructions

Prepare the grill:

Remove neck and giblets from cavity of chicken, Mix the salt, pepper, and thyme in a little bowl, and rub it all over the chicken. Lower chicken onto half-filled beer can:

Make sure the beer can is open, and only half-filled with beer (drink the other half!) If you want, you can put a sprig of thyme, or another herb like rosemary or sage in the beer can for additional flavor.

Lower the chicken on to the open can, so that the chicken is sitting upright, with the can in its cavity.

Grill on indirect heat:

Place the chicken on the cool side of the grill, using the legs and beer can as a tripod to support the chicken and keep it stable.

Cover the grill and walk away. Do not even check the chicken for at least an hour. After an hour, check the chicken and refresh the coals if needed (if you are using a charcoal grill).

Keep checking the chicken every 15 minutes or so, until a meat thermometer inserted into the thickest part of the thigh reads 165°F. A 4-pound chicken will usually take around 1 1/2 hours.

CHAPTER ELEVEN

Chili, Stew, and Other Parking Lot Lifelines

At a certain temperature, grilling becomes optional.

Hot food does not.

This is where chili earns its authority.

Chili does not care about wind. Chili does not panic when the grill sputters. Chili sits patiently in a slow cooker or battered stock pot, radiating warmth and confidence like it has seen worse than this. Which, in Buffalo, it probably has.

These foods exist to stabilize the situation. They warm hands. They slow conversations down just enough. They forgive lateness, distractions, and the fact that nobody remembers exactly when they were started.

If wings are the headline and burgers are the workhorse, chili and stew are the insurance policy. When the weather turns rude or the schedule slips, these dishes quietly save the day.

Below are six full, tailgate-proven recipes designed to survive cold air, long holds, and repeated ladling.

Classic Buffalo Tailgate Chili

Instructions

Brown beef in a large pot. Drain excess fat.

Add onion and garlic, cook until soft.

Stir in spices and salt.

Add beans, tomatoes, and broth.

Simmer 30–40 minutes, stirring occasionally.

Transfer to slow cooker to hold.

Tailgate Law:
Everyone has an opinion. Nobody is wrong until they add sugar.

Ingredients

2 lbs ground beef

1 large onion, diced

2 cloves garlic, minced

2 tablespoons chili powder

1 tablespoon cumin

1 tablespoon paprika

1 tablespoon salt

½ tablespoon black pepper

2 cans kidney beans, drained

1 can crushed tomatoes

1 cup beef broth

Fartless White Chicken Chili

Ingredients

1 pound chicken breasts, boneless skinless, chopped

No Beans

1 medium onion, chopped

1 tablespoon olive oil

2 garlic cloves, minced

28 ounces chicken broth

4 ounces chopped green chilies

2 teaspoons ground cumin

2 teaspoons dried mexican oregano

1/2 teaspoons cayenne pepper

1 teaspoon chili powder

1 cup shredded Monterey Jack cheese

Chopped jalapeno pepper

Instructions

Cook chicken and onion in oil until lightly browned in a Dutch oven over medium heat.

Add garlic and cook for another minute.

Stir in the broth, chilies, cumin, oregano and cayenne; bring to a boil.

Reduce heat to low. Simmer for 20-30 minutes or until chicken is no longer pink and onion is tender.

Top each serving with cheese and jalapeno pepper.

Tailgate Law:
If you still have gas after eating this, blame the beer

South Buffalo Irish Stew

Instructions

Heat oil in a large skillet over medium heat until hot. Add onion, celery and garlic; cook and stir 3 minutes or until tender. Remove vegetables with slotted spoon to a small bowl.

Arrange chicken in single layer in skillet. Cook over medium-high heat 5 minutes per side or until lightly browned.

Add onion, celery, garlic, carrots, parsnips, potatoes, thyme, salt and pepper to the skillet. Pour stout over chicken and vegetables. Bring to a boil over high heat. Reduce heat to low. Cover and simmer 35 minutes.

Add mushrooms and corn to skillet. Cover and cook 10 minutes. Then uncover skillet; increase heat to medium. Cook 10 minutes longer or until sauce is slightly reduced and chicken is no longer pink in center.

Ingredients

2 tablespoon vegetable oil

1 medium onion, chopped

2 large garlic cloves, minced

2 stalks celery, chopped

2 young parsnips, peeled and chopped

2 pounds boneless, skinless chicken breasts and thighs, cut into chunks

5 carrots, peeled and chopped

2 parsnips, peeled and chopped

4 large potatoes, peeled and chopped

1 teaspoon dried thyme leaves

3/4 teaspoon salt

1/2 teaspoon black pepper

12 oz Guinness Stout

1/2 lb button mushrooms

Level-Up Brisket Chili

Ingredients

6 slices thick-cut bacon, cut crosswise into 1/2-inch pieces

1 (4 to 5pound) brisket, trimmed and cut into 1/2-inch pieces

2 teaspoons salt, divided

3 dried ancho chiles, seeds and stems removed, chopped

1 large white or yellow onion, finely diced (about 2 cups)

2 canned chipotle peppers in adobo sauce, finely chopped

6 cloves garlic, finely grated or minced

3 tablespoons chili powder

2 tablespoons tomato paste

2 teaspoons freshly ground black pepper, plus more as needed

2 teaspoons smoked paprika

1/4 teaspoon ground cinnamon

1 (12-ounce) bottle dark beer, such

3 tablespoons masa harina

1 (32-ounce) carton beef or chicken broth (4 cups)

Instructions

Place bacon slices in a large Dutch oven or heavy-bottomed pot and cook over medium-low heat until browned and crisp, 8 to 10 minutes. Transfer the bacon to a paper towel-lined plate.

Increase the heat to medium-high. Season chopped brisket all over with 1 teaspoon of the kosher salt. Working in 3 batches, add the brisket to the pot in a single layer and sear undisturbed until the bottom develops a dark brown crust. Stir and continue cooking until browned all over, about 4 minutes more. Using tongs or a slotted spoon, transfer to a large plate. Repeat searing the remaining brisket and transferring to the plate.

Reduce the heat to medium-low. Add dried ancho chiles and onion to the pot. Scrape up any browned bits from the bottom of the pot and cook until the onion is softened and browned, about 5 minutes.

Stir in chipotle peppers in adobo sauce, garlic cloves, chili powder, tomato paste, brown sugar, cumin, black pepper, smoked paprika, cinnamon, and the remaining kosher salt. Cook, stirring constantly, until fragrant and lightly toasted, about 1 minute.

Stir in dark beer and masa harina, and repeat scraping up the browned bits from the bottom of the pot. Pour in beef broth and crushed tomatoes. Return the bacon and beef and any accumulated juices on the plate to the pot and stir to combine. Bring to a simmer. Reduce the heat to low.

Partially cover and simmer, stirring every 20 minutes or so, until the beef is fork-tender but not falling apart, 2 to 2 1/2 hours. Taste and season with more kosher salt and black pepper as needed.

Chicken Corn Chowder

Cook bacon in large pot over medium-high heat until crisp. Using slotted spoon, transfer bacon to paper towels to drain. Pour off all but 1/4 cup drippings from pot.

Add butter to pot and sauté onions and bell peppers over medium-high heat until soft, about 10 minutes. Slowly add flour and stir for 2 minutes.

Mix in broth, potatoes, and thyme and bring to a boil. Reduce heat to medium-low; simmer uncovered until potatoes are tender, about 10 minutes.

Add corn, chicken, reserved bacon, and cream and simmer until corn is tender, about 10 minutes.

10 bacon slices, chopped

2 tablespoons butter (1/4 stick)

3 medium onions, chopped

2 cups diced red bell peppers

1/4 cup all purpose flour

9 cups chicken broth

1-1/2 pounds Russet potatoes, cut into 1/2-inch cubes

1-1/2 tablespoons thyme, chopped

2 16-ounce bags frozen corn

1 Rotisserie chicken, shredded

1 cup heavy cream

Salt and pepper to taste

Cajun Chicken & Sausage Gumbo

1 cup vegetable oil

1 cup all-purpose flour

1 large onion, chopped

1 large green bell pepper, chopped

2 celery stalks, chopped

1 pound andouille sausage, sliced 1/4 inch thick

4 cloves garlic, minced

Salt and pepper to taste

Creole seasoning to taste

6 cups chicken broth

1 bay leaf

1 rotisserie chicken, boned and shredded

Heat vegetable oil in a Dutch oven over medium heat and whisk in flour. Continue whisking 8 to 10 minutes until the roux has cooked to the color of chocolate milk. Be very careful not to burn the roux. If you see black specks in the mixture, start over.

Stir onion, bell pepper, celery, and sausage into the roux; cook 5 minutes. Stir in the garlic and cook another 5 minutes. Season with salt, pepper, and Creole seasoning.

Pour in the chicken broth and add the bay leaf. Bring to a boil over high heat, then reduce heat to medium-low, and simmer, uncovered, for 1 hour, stirring occasionally.

Add in the chicken, and simmer for another hour.

CHAPTER TWELVE
The Sacred Dip Table

Every Buffalo tailgate has a center of gravity.

It is not the grill.

It is not the cooler.

It is the dip table.

The dip table is where people gather without admitting they're gathering. It's where conversations start, restart, and quietly continue long after the main food is "almost ready." It requires no utensils, no commitment, and no explanation. You hover. You scoop. You nod.

Dips are democratic. They don't care when you arrived, how cold you are, or what you're wearing. They exist to keep hands busy and spirits level while the rest of the operation catches up.

A proper Buffalo dip table follows a few unspoken rules:

- At least one dip must be hot.
- At least one dip must contain dairy.
- At least one dip must disappear faster than expected.
- No dip should require instructions.

Below are six full, tailgate-tested dip recipes that hold the line from setup to kickoff.

Chicken Wing Dip *(Mandatory)*

Instructions

In a large saucepan over medium-high heat, combine chicken and hot sauce. Stir in cream cheese, Ranch dressing, and shredded cheese. Continue to stir until hot and bubbly, about 5 minutes.

Transfer to a fondue pot or slow cooker to keep warm.

Serve with celery sticks and toast tips.

Ingredients

4 cups cooked chicken, shredded

1/4 cup Frank's Hot Sauce

2- 8 ounce packages cream cheese

1 cup Ranch salad dressing

2 cups shredded cheddar cheese

1 bunch celery, trimmed and cut into 4-inch pieces, for serving

Toast tips for serving

Cheeseburger Dip

Ingredients

1 tablespoon .vegetable oil

1 lbs. ground sirloin

1 tablespoon Worcestershire sauce

1 teaspoon kosher salt

1 tteaspoon ground black pepper

12 oz cream cheese, softened

1 (8-oz.) bag shredded cheddar jack cheese, divided

1 cup thinly sliced lettuce

1/2 cup diced tomato

1/4 cup diced red onion

1/4 cup chopped dill pickle

Kettle cooked potato chips

1/3 cup mayonnaise

1 tablespoon mustard

1 1/2 tablespoons ketchup

1/4 teaspoon garlic powder

1/4 teaspoon onion powder

1/4 teaspoon smoked paprika

1 tablespoon pickle juice

(from the jar)

Instructions

Preheat the oven to 375°F.

In a medium skillet, heat the oil over medium-high heat. Add the ground beef, Worcestershire, salt, and pepper. Cook, using a wooden spoon to break the beef into small pieces, until lightly browned and no longer pink, about 6 minutes. Remove from the heat.

Spread the cream cheese to fill the bottom of a 10-inch cast-iron skillet. Top with half of the shredded cheese, the cooked ground beef, and the remaining shredded cheese on top. Bake until the edges are bubbly, 18 to 20 minutes. Let cool slightly, about 10 minutes.

In a small bowl, stir together the mayonnaise, mustard, ketchup, garlic and onion powders, smoked paprika, and pickle brine.

Top the dip with lettuce, tomato, red onion, and pickle. Drizzle with the special sauce. Serve with kettle-cooked potato chips or pita chips.

Hot Spinach Artichoke Dip

Instructions

Mix all ingredients thoroughly.

Transfer to foil pan.

Heat until melted and bubbling.

Stir once and serve hot.

Tailgate Law:

This convinces people to stay longer than planned.

Ingredients

8 oz cream cheese, softened

1/2 cup sour cream

1/2 cup mayonnaise

1 cup shredded mozzarella

1/2 cup grated Parmesan

1 cup chopped spinach

1 cup chopped artichoke hearts

Guacamole

Ingredients

1/4 cup lime juice

1/4 cup chopped red onion

1 teaspoon .kosher salt

4 whole ripe avocados

1/2 cup diced tomato

1/4 cup chopped cilantro

1 jalapeño, seeded and diced

Tortilla chips and fresh veggies, for serving

Instructions

In a medium bowl, combine the lime juice, onion, and salt. Let sit for 5 minutes.

Halve the avocados lengthwise and remove the pits.

Using a spoon, scrape the flesh of the avocado into the bowl with the onion mixture.

Mash the avocados, making sure to leave it relatively chunky.

Add the tomatoes, cilantro, and jalapeño and stir together.

Serve with tortilla chips and fresh veggies for dipping.

Blue Cheese Dip

Instructions

Gently.stir all ingredients together

Chill if possible, though it rarely lasts that long.

Serve with celery or chips.

Tailgate Law:

Chunks must be visible from space.

Smooth is suspicious.

Ingredients

1 cup sour cream

1/2 cup mayonnaise

1/2 cup crumbled blue cheese

1 teaspoon lemon juice

Black pepper to taste

Seven-Layer Dip

Ingredients

1 can refried beans

1 cup sour cream

1 cup guacamole

1 cup salsa

1½ cups shredded Mexican-blend cheese

1/2 cup chopped tomatoes

1/4 cup sliced green onions

Instructions

Spread beans evenly in a wide dish.

Layer sour cream, guacamole, and salsa.

Sprinkle with cheese, tomatoes, and green onions.

Serve immediately.

Tailgate Law:

Someone will dig straight to the bottom.

This is expected.

CHAPTER THIRTEEN
Classic Tailgate Game Changers

Some foods don't just feed a tailgate.

They change its posture.

These are the dishes that make people stop wandering and start circling. The ones that pull conversations inward, extend stays, and convince someone who planned to "just say hi" to cancel the rest of their morning. They're reliable, scalable, and emotionally effective.

Game changers don't need babysitting. They hold heat. They forgive delays. They taste even better when eaten standing up with a plastic fork that may or may not survive the encounter.

What follows are eight certified Buffalo tailgate game changers. Make one and you're helpful. Make two and you're important. Make three and people ask where you're setting up next week.

Game changers don't announce themselves.

They just empty.

When the slow cooker's scraped clean, the fries vanish, and someone asks for the recipe you

didn't bring written down, you've done your job.

The tailgate has shifted.

People are staying.

And the day feels possible.

Philly-Style Shedded Beef Sliders

Instructions

Season beef on all sides.

Place beef, peppers, onions, and broth in slow cooker.

Cook on LOW 8 hours or HIGH 4–5 hours.

Shred beef and return to juices.

Assemble sliders with beef and provolone.

Cover briefly to melt cheese.

Tailgate Law:

Nobody eats just one.

Ingredients

3 lbs beef chuck roast

1 teaspoon salt

1 teaspoon black pepper

1 teaspoon garlic powder

1 teaspoon onion powder

1 green bell pepper, sliced

1 onion, sliced

2 cups beef broth

12 slider rolls

12 slices provolone cheese

Pulled Pork Sliders

Ingredients

4 lbs pork shoulder

1 tablespoon paprika

1 tablespoon brown sugar

1 teaspoon salt

1 teaspoon pepper

1 teaspoon garlic powder

1 cup BBQ sauce

12 slider buns

Instructions

Rub pork with all seasonings.

Cook in slow cooker on LOW 8 hours or HIGH 5 hours.

Shred pork, mix with BBQ sauce.

Serve warm on buns.

Optional:
Add coleslaw if you enjoy debates.

Loaded Fries

Instructions

Bake fries until deeply crispy.

Transfer to foil pan.

Top with cheese and bacon.

Cover briefly until cheese melts.

Finish with green onions.

Tailgate Law:

Fries must be eaten immediately or defended aggressively.

Ingredients

3 lbs frozen French fries

2 cups shredded cheddar

1 cup cooked bacon, chopped

1/2 cup green onions

Sour cream (optional)

Spicy Chex™ Mix

Ingredients

3 cups Rice Chex™

3 cups Corn Chex™

2 cups pretzels

1 cup mixed nuts

1/2 cup melted butter

2 tablespoon hot sauce

1 teaspoon garlic powder

1 teaspoon smoked paprika

Instructions

Mix dry ingredients in large bowl.

Stir butter, hot sauce, and spices together.

Toss evenly.

Bake at 250°F for 1 hour, stirring every 15 minutes.

Tailgate Law:

Someone will eat this without realizing how much.

Dill Pickle Ranch Potato Salad

Instructions

Boil potatoes until tender. Cool completely.

Mix remaining ingredients.

Fold potatoes gently into dressing.

Chill before serving.

Tailgate Law:

This converts skeptics without warning.

Ingredients

3 lbs red potatoes, cubed

1 cup ranch dressing

1/2 cup sour cream

1 cup chopped dill pickles

1/4 cup pickle juice

Salt and pepper to taste

Tater Tot Nachos

Ingredients

1 1/2 tablespoon onion powder

1 teaspoon. garlic powder

1 teaspoon ground black pepper

1 (28-ounce) bag frozen tater tots

1 lb. chorizo, casings removed, finely chopped

1 small yellow onion, diced small (about 1 cup)

12 oz. processed cheese (such as Velveeta), cut into large cubes

1 (10-ounce) can diced tomatoes and green chiles

1 (4-ounce) can chopped green chiles

1 jalapeño, thinly sliced

Fresh cilantro, coarsely chopped, for serving

Instructions

Preheat the oven to 425°F. Line a rimmed baking sheet with parchment paper. .

In a small bowl, combine the onion powder, garlic powder, and black pepper. Spread out the tater tots on the prepared baking sheet, sprinkle over the spice mixture, and toss to evenly coat. Spread the tater tots in an even layer and bake until crispy.

Add the chorizo and yellow onion to a large, nonstick skillet set over medium-high heat. Cook until the chorizo is browned and the onion is translucent.

Drain off any excess fat. Return to medium-high heat and add the processed cheese, tomatoes with green chiles, and the chopped green chiles. Stir to combine and reduce the heat to low. Cook, stirring occasionally, until the cheese is melted and the queso is hot.

Pour a layer of queso over the tater tots. Top with some of the jalapeño slices, pickled red onions, and cilantro.

Crockpot Mac & Cheese

Instructions

In a 6 to 8-quart slow-cooker, stir together the macaroni, whole milk, evaporated milk, heavy cream, butter, salt, pepper, paprika, and cayenne.

Cover and cook on high for 30 minutes. Stir the mixture, cover, and cook until the noodles are almost tender, about 25 minutes more. (Check the noodles—if they are still too firm, continue to cook in 10 minute increments until they are tender, with a slight bite.)

With the slow cooker still on high heat, add the American cheese, gently folding it into the macaroni with a rubber spatula until almost melted. Working in three batches, gently fold in the cheddar and gouda, making sure the cheese is fully melted before adding the next batch.

Serve immediately, or set the slow cooker to warm for up to 2 hours. (When holding the mac and cheese on warm for serving, gently stir occasionally and fold in 2 tablespoons of warm milk, as needed, to loosen the sauce.)

Ingredients

1- 16-oz. box elbow macaroni

2 1/2 cups whole milk, plus more for serving

1- 12-oz. can evaporated milk

1/2 cup heavy cream

4 tablespoons unsalted butter

1 teaspoon kosher salt

1/2 teaspoon.ground black pepper

1/4 teaspoon.paprika

1/8 teaspoon cayenne

1/4 lb. American cheese, cubed

1- 8-oz. bag shredded sharp cheddar cheese

1 cup shredded smoked gouda cheese

Sloppy Joes

Ingredients

2 tablespoon butter, plus more for the rolls

2 1/2 lb. ground beef

5 garlic cloves, minced

1 large green bell pepper, diced

1/2 large onion, diced

1 teaspoon kosher salt

1/2 teaspoon black pepper

1 1/2 cups ketchup

2 tablespoons brown sugar

1 tablespoon Worcestershire sauce

2 teaspoon chili powder, plus more to taste

1 teaspoon dry mustard

1/2 teaspoon crushed red pepper flakes, plus more to taste

8 kaiser rolls, split

8 slices cheese (such as cheddar, American, pepper jack; optional)

Instructions

In a large skillet, melt the butter over medium-high heat. Add the ground beef and cook, breaking up the meat with a wooden spoon, until browned, 5 to 7 minutes. Drain off and discard most of the fat.

Add the garlic, bell pepper, onion, salt, and black pepper and cook, stirring occasionally, until the vegetables begin to soften, 5 to 7 minutes. Pour the mixture into a 6-quart slow cooker.

Add the ketchup, brown sugar, Worcestershire sauce, chili powder, dry mustard, red pepper flakes, and ½ cup water. Stir to combine.

Cook until the flavors concentrate and the mixture reduces slightly and deepens in color around the edges, on high for 2 hours or low for 4 hours. Taste and adjust the seasonings as needed.

Spoon the meat mixture (about ½ cup) over each roll, topping with slices of cheese, if you like.

Serve with hot sauce, chips, and a pickle.

CHAPTER FOURTEEN
Beer Is the Default Setting

In Buffalo tailgating, beverages are not an accessory.

They are infrastructure.

Beer appears early, not because anyone is rushing, but because it establishes baseline reality. Once a can is opened, the day officially begins. Before that, you're just standing around in layers, talking about the drive in.

Beer does several important jobs at once. It warms hands. It slows time. It lowers the volume on unnecessary analysis. It gives people something to do while waiting for food, friends, or the confidence to say what they've been thinking since Tuesday.

The first beer is rarely dramatic. It's practical. A quiet acknowledgment that you're here and not going anywhere.

Cold weather changes the rules. In Buffalo, beer temperature exists on a sliding scale. Ice-cold is acceptable early. Cool is ideal. Frozen is a logistics failure that will be discussed openly and without mercy. Veterans know better than to leave cans on the ground. Snow is not a cooler. It is a trap.

Cans dominate the scene for obvious reasons. They open easily. They don't shatter. They survive being dropped, kicked, or briefly forgotten in a snowbank. Bottles show up occasionally, but they carry risk. Anyone holding one is watched carefully.

You'll notice that beer choices follow an unspoken hierarchy. Light beers lead. Local brews appear next, usually accompanied by commentary. Something seasonal shows up and is debated politely. No one judges. The important thing is volume and availability, not curation.

Beer is shared freely. Nobody keeps count. If you run out, someone hands you another without ceremony. This is not generosity. It's maintenance. A tailgate with uneven beer distribution becomes unstable quickly.

At some point, someone cracks a beer they've been saving "for the game." This is symbolic. It means time has shifted. Kickoff is close. Conversations tighten. The playlist gets louder. People start looking toward the stadium more often.

Beer also functions as emotional ballast. It smooths optimism. It cushions disappointment. It gives people permission to laugh at things they've already overthought all week. It doesn't erase nerves, but it keeps them from running the show.

Importantly, beer does not accelerate the day. It stretches it. Sips replace glances at the clock. One more turns into enough. Enough turns into just right.

There is always someone who switches to water at the correct moment. They are respected. They are not questioned. They understand the long game.

Eventually, the coolers close. Lids latch with finality. Leftover cans are redistributed. The walk toward the stadium begins.

Beer has done its work.

Hands are warm. Voices are steady. The edge has softened just enough.

The default setting has been restored.

Next chapter, we'll talk about the other beverages. The ones poured carefully, offered quietly, and remembered later for reasons that are never fully documented.

CHAPTER FIFTEEN
Shots, Thermoses, and Questionable Decisions

Beer sets the tone.

Everything else changes the temperature.

If beer is the default setting, then the harder stuff is the fine adjustment knob. It's not for everyone. It's not always necessary. But it is always present, tucked discreetly into coat pockets, backpacks, and thermoses that have clearly never held coffee.

These beverages arrive without announcements. No labels. No back story beyond, "You want some?" This is how trust is tested in Buffalo parking lots.

Shots appear early but not immediately. Too soon and you raise concerns. Too late and you miss the window. Timing matters. The first round usually coincides with a successful grill moment, a friend arriving late, or someone announcing, "We've got time."

Shot glasses are rare. Plastic cups are common. Bottle caps double as measurement tools. Precision is less important than intent.

What's inside varies. Whiskey dominates, for reasons no one questions. Something cinnamon-flavored appears and vanishes quickly. There is always one bottle that came from someone's cousin or basement and defies classification. It smells strong. It tastes stronger. It will be remembered.

Thermoses deserve special recognition. They are the unsung heroes of cold-weather tailgating. Stainless steel cylinders filled with liquids designed to warm from the inside out. Coffee is the cover story. The truth emerges by the second sip.

Thermos culture follows strict etiquette:
- Never ask what's in it first.
- Always take a small sip before committing.
- Compliment it, regardless of outcome.

This is not politeness. It is survival.

There is a brief window where these drinks feel like a great idea. The cold recedes. Laughter gets louder. Stories become shorter and more confident. The weather feels personal again, in a good way.

Then the window closes.

Experienced tailgaters recognize the signs. The volume rises just a little too much. Gloves come off unnecessarily. Someone suggests moving locations. This is when the thermos quietly goes back into the car.

Questionable decisions are part of the ecosystem, but they are managed. Buffalo tailgating is not reckless. It is self-regulating. Someone always steps in. Someone always hands over water. Someone always says, "Save that for after."

Because there is still a game to attend.

The goal is warmth, not amnesia. Camaraderie, not chaos. You want to remember how you felt walking into the stadium, not wonder how you got there.

When done right, these drinks don't derail the day. They add texture. They become footnotes in conversations that start with, "Remember that time when–" and end in laughter.

By the time kickoff nears, the bottles are sealed, the thermoses are capped, and the mood settles.

Beer returns to the lead role.

The edges smooth out.

The decisions stop being questionable.

That's when you know it worked.

CHAPTER SIXTEEN

The Grill You've Had Since Clinton Was President

Every Buffalo tailgate has a grill.

And every grill has a back story.

It might be rusted. It might lean slightly to the left. One knob may have snapped off sometime during the late nineties and been replaced with pliers that are now considered a permanent feature. None of this matters. In fact, it's preferred.

New grills are suspicious. Old grills are trusted.

The grill you've had since Clinton was president has earned its place. It has survived rain, snow, road salt, and more than one season that tested your emotional stability. It lights when it wants to, not when you ask, and it responds best to encouragement and patience.

This grill has seen things.

It has cooked burgers at dawn and sausages long after anyone remembers who brought them. It has warmed hands, deflected wind, and served as a gathering point for conversations that started about football and ended somewhere else entirely.

You don't clean this grill. You maintain it. There is a difference.

Maintenance involves scraping when absolutely necessary, replacing parts only after a proper debate, and refusing to admit how many years it's been since the drip tray was last emptied. This is not neglect. It's seasoning.

Every experienced tailgater knows that grills develop personalities. Some run hot. Some refuse to cooperate below freezing. Some flare up unexpectedly, just to remind you who's in charge. Learning these quirks takes time. That time is part of the investment.

When someone offers to bring a brand-new grill, the group hesitates. Not because it won't work, but because it hasn't proven itself. Trust is earned one frozen ignition at a time.

The grill also establishes hierarchy. Whoever brought it, tends it. Advice is offered freely, but authority rests with the owner. You may suggest adjustments. You may not take over.

Grills attract people. They draw clusters of fans who claim they're just warming up but stay for twenty minutes. They become landmarks. "We're by the old Weber" is a complete set of directions.

At some point, the grill will misbehave. The flame will dip. The wind will interfere. Someone will bang the side gently, as if that helps. It usually does.

When food finally comes off, hot and imperfect, the grill earns another season of service. Nobody questions it. Nobody replaces it. It will be packed up carefully, as if it's fragile, even though it clearly isn't.

Because this grill isn't just equipment. It's continuity.

It shows up every week, regardless of record or forecast. It does its job without complaint. It reminds everyone that some things don't need upgrading.

As long as the grill fires up, the tailgate will happen.

And if it doesn't?

Someone nearby has another one that's almost as old.

Next chapter, we move from fire to furniture. Tables, chairs, and the structural myths that briefly hold everything together.

CHAPTER SEVENTEEN
The Sound System Arms Race

At some point, silence becomes suspicious.

Buffalo tailgating does not require music, but it improves with it. The moment a speaker clicks on, the tailgate announces itself. Not just to nearby rows, but to the entire lot. This is territory marking through sound.

The escalation happens slowly. One small speaker at first, just loud enough to cut through the wind. Then another tailgate answers. Then someone upgrades. By mid-morning, the parking lot hums with overlapping playlists that somehow work together.

Volume is important, but confidence matters more.

A sound system doesn't need to be expensive. It needs to be loud enough to survive open space, cold air, and someone yelling over it. The best systems are slightly battered, wrapped in duct tape, and carried like they've been here before.

The music itself follows a recognizable arc. Early on, it's background. Something steady. Familiar. Then the tempo rises. By the time the grill is hot and the beer is flowing, the playlist locks into classics that everyone knows whether they admit it or not.

No one curates in real time. The playlist is trusted. Skipping tracks is frowned upon. Arguing about songs is allowed, but only if you sing along anyway.

Every tailgate has that one person who takes the speaker personally. They stand near it. Adjust it often. Defend it fiercely. This is not ego. It is stewardship.

At a certain point, the arms race peaks. Someone brings out a speaker that should require a permit. The bass travels through the asphalt. Conversations pause. Heads turn. Respect is paid.

Then balance is restored. The volume drops slightly. People move closer together. The music becomes glue instead of a challenge.

Cold air does something strange to sound. It carries farther. It sharpens edges. Laughter and music drift across rows and blend into something larger than any single tailgate. This is how strangers find each other. This is how groups merge.

Eventually, someone says, "We should start packing up." The speaker stays on a little longer. One more song. Always one more.

When the system finally powers down, the silence feels heavier than before. It's not absence. It's anticipation.

Music has done its job. It has filled the space. It has set the tempo. It has reminded everyone that this isn't just waiting.

It's participation.

Next chapter, we meet the people. The regulars, the legends, and the personalities who turn parking lots into neighborhoods.

CHAPTER EIGHTEEN

The Regulars, the Newcomer, and the Keeper of Memory

Every Buffalo tailgate looks chaotic from the outside.

From the inside, it's a system.

That system works because three kinds of people always show up, whether they planned to or not.

First, there is the Mayor of the Parking Lot.

The Mayor did not volunteer. The role simply found them. They arrive early enough that the lot still feels theoretical. By the time others arrive, the Mayor already knows who's late, who forgot plates, and who is parking too close to the grill.

The Mayor moves constantly. They do not sit. Sitting would suggest the job is done, which it never is. They introduce people who didn't know they needed introductions. They redirect food before it becomes a problem. They say things like "We'll put that here" in a tone that somehow makes everyone agree.

The Mayor may or may not have a ticket. This is irrelevant. Their authority ends at the stadium gate because it does not need to go further.

Then there is the First-Timer.

You can spot them instantly. They are underdressed in a way that feels hopeful. They stand slightly too straight. They ask questions that make sense elsewhere. "Is it always like this?" "What time do people usually show up?" "Are people really going to do that?"

Yes.

Earlier.

And yes again.

The First-Timer does not know the rules yet, but the system is kind to them. Food appears in their hands without paperwork. Someone explains something they didn't ask about but will later repeat as fact. Their jacket gets marked with sauce or snow or both, which is how admission is processed.

Within an hour, they change. Their voice gets louder. Their stance widens. They stop apologizing for being in the way. By the second plate, they are no longer observing. They are participating.

They will say, "Next time I'll bring –" before realizing there is already a next time.

And then there is the Historian.

The Historian remembers everything.

Not just scores, but conditions. The wind that day. The way the crowd sounded. The call that still doesn't sit right. These memories are delivered precisely, without notes, often when nobody asked but everyone needed it.

The Historian does not dominate conversation. They time it. They know when optimism needs restraint and when disappointment needs perspective. They remind people that this feeling has existed before and did not end anything important.

They are not pessimistic. They are careful.

Together, these three keep the tailgate balanced.

The Mayor keeps it running.

The First-Timer keeps it alive.

The Historian keeps it grounded.

Without one, something tilts. With all three present, the parking lot becomes what it always becomes: a temporary neighborhood that works better than it has any right to.

By the time kickoff approaches, the Mayor steps back, the First-Timer feels strangely confident, and the Historian nods once, as if the day has been properly accounted for.

Nothing needs to be said.

The system is working.

CHAPTER NINETEEN
The Same Spot, Every Time
(And Why It Matters Where You Stand)

There is a place in the parking lot that belongs to you.

Not spiritually. Literally.

In Buffalo, tailgating geography is not casual. It's inherited, defended, and quietly respected. You don't just park anywhere and expect the universe to cooperate. You return to your spot. Or you deal with the consequences.

Some people swear by Hammer Lot.

The Hammer Lot does not advertise itself. It doesn't need to. If you know, you know. It's where intensity concentrates. Where grills fire up early, flags fly high, and volume is treated like a moral obligation. The Hammer Lot is not for warming up. It is for arriving ready.

People here don't ask if it's too early. They ask where you've been.

Then there's the pull of the Twin Oaks Motel.

Calling it a motel undersells it. Twin Oaks is less a place to stay and more a long-running pregame institution with a motel. Tailgating here happens with purpose. Tables line up with confidence. Generators hum. The rhythm is familiar enough that you can show up and immediately know where not to stand.

Twin Oaks regulars do not drift. They arrive, set up, and hold court. You don't wander into this space accidentally. You are either invited or absorbed.

And then there is the gravitational pull of the Red Zone.

The Red Zone is movement. It's flow. It's where groups overlap, merge, split, and reconnect. It's louder than you expect and friendlier than it looks. This is where first-timers get baptized and veterans make rounds.

The Red Zone is less about permanence and more about energy. You may not set up there every week, but you pass through. Everyone does. It's how news travels. It's how stories start.

What all these places have in common is memory.

You remember what happened there. Not just games, but moments. Snowfall that changed plans. A win that felt different. A loss that required an extra layer of chili. Over time, the spot absorbs those experiences. Returning feels like alignment.

Parking somewhere else introduces doubt. The wind hits wrong. The grill faces the wrong direction. Conversations take longer to settle. You'll say it's fine, but you won't mean it.

The same spot removes friction. It lets the day unfold the way it's supposed to. You know where the sun will be, if the sun decides to participate. You know where people will gather. You know where to look when someone says, "Did you hear?"

By the time kickoff approaches, the location has done half the work. The ritual holds. The group steadies. You pack up with the satisfaction that comes from doing things the right way, in the right place.

It's not superstition.

It's familiarity with consequences.

CHAPTER TWENTY
Porta-Potties: A Study of Faith and Timing

No tailgate plan survives first contact with the porta-potty.

You can bring the right food.

You can dress correctly.

You can arrive early, park perfectly, and execute the grill like a professional.

Eventually, you will still have to reckon with the plastic tower.

Porta-potties at tailgates are not amenities. They are tests. Of judgment. Of patience. Of how badly you really want that next beer.

They appear in neat rows early in the morning, clean enough to inspire optimism. Doors closed. Floors intact. Blue liquid calm and unthreatening. At this stage, people walk past them confidently, telling themselves they'll "go later."

This is a mistake, because porta-potties age in dog years.

By mid-morning, usage patterns begin to reveal themselves. Certain units become popular for reasons no one can fully explain. Others are quietly abandoned after a single traumatic visit. Veterans take note. They remember numbers. They share intel in hushed tones.

Timing becomes everything. Early is safest. Immediately after arrival is ideal. Waiting until after the chili is risky. Waiting until after the margaritas is an act of faith that has ended friendships.

Lines form without warning. They are never straight. They drift. They hesitate. They collapse inward like something alive. Conversations happen here that do not happen anywhere else. Eye contact is brief. Solidarity is implied.

Inside, expectations are adjusted quickly.

You do not judge.

You do not linger.

You do not look down longer than necessary.

You focus. You commit. You exit with dignity, or at least the appearance of it.

There are rules, though they are never written.

You knock, even if you're sure it's empty.

You lock the door every time.

You never comment on what you encountered inside.

Silence is kindness.

And then there are the elevated porta-potty stories. The ones involving people climbing onto them, standing near them, or using them as platforms for enthusiasm. These stories spread faster than facts and are always told with the same mix of disbelief and pride.

The porta-potty endures it all.

It takes abuse. It absorbs chaos. It stands quietly while the rest of the tailgate loses its balance. It is not thanked. It is not respected. But it is essential.

By late afternoon, no one is pretending anymore. The remaining units are chosen strategically, like a last slice of pizza. People approach with resolve. They come back changed.

And yet, no one leaves early because of them.

Because tailgating is about accepting conditions as they are, not as you wish them to be.
The porta-potty is part of that agreement. An imperfect solution that allows everything else to continue.

You survive it.

You laugh about it later.

You return next week knowing exactly when to go.

That's growth.

That's experience.

CHAPTER TWENTY ONE
Flags and Moveable Art

Decoration at a Buffalo tailgate is not about aesthetics.

It's about identification.

You're not trying to impress anyone. You're trying to be found. In a parking lot that looks the same in every direction, flags, cars, and the occasional rolling spectacle exist to say: we are here, and we are not subtle about it.

It starts with flags.

A proper tailgate flag is large enough to create drag. It whips. It snaps. It makes noise even when nobody's talking. Mounted to trucks, poles, tents, or things that were never designed to hold flags, it serves as both beacon and warning. Flags are raised early. Lowering them early feels wrong. Wind damage is accepted as part of the lifecycle.

A flag with frayed edges has credibility. A pristine flag suggests this might be your first time.

Cars are next.

Vehicles become canvases. Window flags appear. Magnets slap onto doors with confidence. Decals layer over previous seasons like archaeological evidence. Someone has a hood painted blue and red. Someone else regrets not checking the weather before sticking something on permanently.

Tailgate cars are not washed before games. That would erase history. Road salt, sauce splatter, and the occasional mystery streak are left intact. These are not flaws. They are documentation.

Then there are the trucks.

Pickup beds become stages. Speakers live here. People stand here. Occasionally people jump from here into tables, which is not recommended but rarely discouraged. Trucks with open tailgates act like town squares. Everything radiates outward.

And then, once in a while, there is a bus.

Not a shuttle.

Not a rental.

A bus.

School bus. Coach bus. Former church bus. The kind of vehicle that required planning, paint, and the confidence to think, "Yes, this is reasonable."

Paint jobs are never subtle. Red. Blue. Logos. Slogans. Sometimes flames, because someone got excited. The inside is reimagined entirely. Seats removed. Coolers installed. TVs wired in ways that suggest a background in either engineering or optimism.

The bus does not move much. It doesn't need to. It is the destination.

People gravitate toward it without asking. Photos are taken. Stories start there. You may not know who owns it, but you respect them immediately.

Decoration escalates throughout the morning. More flags go up. More magnets appear. Someone ties something to a pole that definitely shouldn't be tied there. Nobody intervenes.

Because decoration isn't clutter here. It's communication.

It says: this group planned. This group committed. This group will not quietly disappear after the game.

When kickoff approaches, nothing is taken down. Flags stay flying. Cars remain marked. The bus remains exactly where it is, humming softly, as if guarding the lot.

Because these decorations aren't for the game.

They're for each other.

So people can find their way back.

So the place still feels claimed.

So next week, when someone says, "Same spot," they know exactly what that means.

If you can see the flags, you're home.

CHAPTER TWENTY TWO
Lucky Gear and Unlucky Comments

Buffalo tailgating does not believe in superstition.

It believes in patterns.

Lucky gear appears early. The same hat. The same jersey. The same jacket that should have been retired but wasn't because good things happened while wearing it. These items are not washed casually. They are treated with restraint and quiet respect.

If something worked once, it deserves another chance.

Unlucky comments, however, are dealt with immediately.

You do not say "This should be easy."

You do not say "We've got this."

You do not say "They're not that good."

If you do, someone will correct you. Gently, but firmly. Not out of fear, but out of experience.

There are also moments when silence is required. During pre-game analysis. During certain songs. During walks toward the stadium. These pauses are not awkward. They are intentional.

Gear is adjusted carefully. Gloves removed and replaced. Hats straightened. Zippers checked twice. These actions feel small, but they carry weight.

None of this guarantees anything. Everyone knows that.

But it creates alignment. It tells the day you're paying attention.

By the time kickoff arrives, the spot is secure, the gear is set, and the comments have been carefully filtered.

You've done everything you can.

Now it's up to the game.

CHAPTER TWENTY THREE
Victory Cleanup

Winning changes the temperature of everything.

The weather feels softer. The walk feels shorter. Even the trash bags cooperate. Victory does not eliminate mess, but it reframes it. Cleanup after a win is not a chore. It's a cool-down lap.

Plates are lighter now. Wings are reduced to bones and memories. Someone stares into a nearly empty foil pan like it might explain what just happened. Conversations overlap, repeat, and restart because nobody is ready to leave the feeling yet.

Cleanup happens slowly on purpose.

Someone folds a chair that didn't need folding yet. Someone wipes down a table that will immediately get dirty again. Coolers are repacked with the care usually reserved for valuables. Leftovers are claimed strategically, like trophies.

There is laughter in the process. Loud, loose laughter that spills out of people who have been holding it in for three hours. Strangers congratulate each other. High-fives are exchanged without introductions. For a brief moment, everyone is an expert, a prophet, and a survivor.

Stories form immediately. Not later. Now.
- [a] "That drive."
- "That stop."
- "That call."

They are already becoming legend, shaped and reshaped with each retelling. Facts are flexible. Emotion is not.

The Mayor makes another round. The Historian nods approvingly. The First-Timer looks stunned, as if they just witnessed proof that something this intense can actually pay off.

Eventually, someone says, "Same time next week," and it lands not as a question but as a plan.

The parking lot empties slowly, reluctantly. No one rushes the exit. Why would you? The day is still warm.

Victory cleanup isn't about packing up. It's about sealing the memory properly so it holds until next Sunday.

CHAPTER TWENTY FOUR
Lose Processing

Losing quiets the lot.

Not immediately. There's a delay. The walk back happens in clusters. Conversations are shorter, measured. People keep their gloves on longer than necessary. The grill stays lit, but no one rushes it.

This is not anger. It's assessment.

Loss processing begins with food. Always food. Chili gets ladled again. Someone finds leftover wings and heats them without comment. Eating slows the spin. It gives hands something to do while the mind replays things it can't fix.

The Historian speaks first.

Not loudly. Not dramatically. Just enough to remind everyone that this feeling has existed before and did not end anything important. Context matters now.

Analysis follows, but gently. No shouting. No absolutes. Criticism is phrased carefully, like handling something fragile. Nobody says "season's over." That's not how this works.

Beer consumption shifts. Slower. More deliberate. Someone switches to water and nobody notices because everyone understands.

There are moments of silence. Real ones. They aren't awkward. They're necessary.

Then humor creeps back in. Dry. Self-aware. The kind that acknowledges disappointment without feeding it. Someone makes a joke that lands perfectly because it shouldn't have.

Cleanup after a loss is efficient. Tables are folded decisively. Chairs go away without ceremony. Leftovers are shared generously. No one hoards anything. You don't take much with you after a loss.

But plans still form.

Next week is mentioned. Adjustments are discussed. Arrival times are debated. Someone says, "We'll figure it out," and it sounds true.

Because this is the part outsiders miss.

Win or lose, the tailgate worked.

People showed up. They fed each other. They stood together in weather that didn't ask permission. They turned a parking lot into something that mattered for a few hours.

That doesn't disappear because of a scoreboard.

By the time the last car pulls away, the disappointment has softened into resolve. The grill will be loaded again. The spot will be reclaimed. The same people will return.

Loss processing ends the same way it always does.

With next Sunday already on the calendar.

EPILOGUE
Next Sunday Starts Now
(But First, Victory Monday)

The parking lot empties.

Not all at once. Not cleanly. It thins out in stages, like a tide pulling back and leaving behind faint evidence that something mattered here. A flattened patch of snow. A forgotten fork. One stubborn bottle cap nobody claims.

By the time the last grill cools and the final chair is folded, the day is technically over.

But Buffalo knows better.

Because the tailgate doesn't end when you leave the lot. It follows you home. It rides with you in the car, settles into the couch, and quietly reappears the next morning at work.

That's where Victory Monday lives.

You feel it before you say it. The alarm clock is less aggressive. The coffee tastes better for reasons science refuses to explain. There's a little extra spring in everyone's step, even among people who swear they "don't really follow football."

You nod at coworkers differently.

You smile faster.

You let things slide.

Someone mentions the game in the hallway. Someone else finishes the sentence. Meetings start with better jokes. Emails feel lighter. The city exhales, collectively, without ever announcing it.

You don't need to wear gear for people to know. It's in posture. In tone. In the way Monday doesn't feel like punishment.

And the planning starts immediately.

What worked.

What didn't.

Who's bringing what next time.

How early is too early, really.

This isn't obsession. It's continuity.

Buffalo tailgating isn't about escaping the week. It gives the week its shape. Sunday sets the tone, and Monday carries it forward like a quiet reward for enduring the cold together.

The weather will change.

The roster will change.

The record will change.

But the parking lot will fill again.

With the same confidence. The same rituals. The same grills that refuse to retire. Newcomers will be fed. Old stories will be told like they still need telling.

Someone will stand in the same spot and feel, briefly, like everything is aligned.

That's the real win.

Not just the score. Not just the standings. The shared lift. The communal reset. The way a good Sunday makes the rest of the week walk a little taller.

Next Sunday starts now.

Monday just carries the glow.

TAILGATE PACKING CHECKLIST
(You Will Forget Something Anyway)

This list is not meant to prevent mistakes.

That would be unrealistic.

Its real purpose is to narrow the margin of error and give you something to point at later when you say, "I swear I had that."

Pack early. Pack confidently. Accept that the checklist is aspirational.

THE NON-NEGOTIABLES

These are the things that turn standing in a parking lot into a tailgate.

- ☐ Tickets (physical, digital, screenshots of the digital, screenshots of the screenshots)
- ☐ ID
- ☐ Cash (someone will only take cash)
- ☐ Phone charger or battery pack
- ☐ Trash bags (more than you think)
- ☐ Paper towels
- ☐ Napkins (extra napkins, emergency napkins)

GRILL & FIRE INFRASTRUCTURE

Fire is the point.

- ☐ Grill (tested at least once this decade)
- ☐ Propane or charcoal (confirmed full, not "probably fine")

- ☐ Lighter(s) (plural)
- ☐ Backup lighter (someone will need it)
- ☐ Tongs
- ☐ Spatula
- ☐ Foil (heavy duty, emotionally supportive amounts)
- ☐ Foil pans
- ☐ Heat-resistant gloves
- ☐ Fire extinguisher (that one responsible friend insists on)

FOOD & CONTAINMENT

Everything will be eaten. Faster than planned.

- ☐ Meat (pre-seasoned if you respect your future self)
- ☐ Buns (not crushed)
- ☐ Wings (already split, unless you enjoy parking-lot knife work)
- ☐ Chili or stew (in something that seals)
- ☐ Dips (at least one hot, one cold)
- ☐ Chips (sturdy, not optimistic)
- ☐ Condiments (mustard, ketchup, onions, pickles)
- ☐ Blue cheese (chunks visible from space)
- ☐ Celery (for balance, not belief)

BEVERAGES

Hydration, Buffalo-style.

- ☐ Beer (more than the math suggests)

- ☐ Water (you will thank yourself later)
- ☐ Thermos (contents discussed quietly)
- ☐ Cups (plastic, sacrificial)
- ☐ Bottle opener (even if you "only brought cans")
- ☐ Ice (but not too much, this isn't a picnic)

FURNITURE & STRUCTURAL GAMBLING

Nothing here is permanent.

- ☐ Folding table(s)
- ☐ Folding chair(s)
- ☐ Backup chair (the good one never survives)
- ☐ Table cover or disposable plastic
- ☐ Duct tape (not optional)
- ☐ Zip ties (solve problems you didn't know you'd have)

CLOTHING & SURVIVAL

Dress like you're staying longer than planned.

- ☐ Extra layers
- ☐ Gloves (warm ones + functional ones)
- ☐ Hat(s)
- ☐ Scarf or face covering
- ☐ Hand warmers

- ☐ Waterproof boots
- ☐ Dry socks (quiet luxury)

SOUND & SIGNAL

Because silence is suspicious.

- ☐ Speaker
- ☐ Charging cable
- ☐ Playlist downloaded (cell service will betray you)
- ☐ Flag, banner, or visual marker (so people can find you)

CLEANUP & EXIT STRATEGY

Future You deserves respect.

- ☐ Cooler(s)
- ☐ Zip-top bags for leftovers
- ☐ Disinfecting wipes
- ☐ Gloves for cleanup (different gloves)
- ☐ Paper plates (biodegradable if you're feeling noble)

THE THINGS YOU WILL STILL FORGET

No checklist can save you from this section.

- ☐ One critical condiment
- ☐ The spatula you were holding five minutes ago

A SHORT GLOSSARY OF PARKING LOT PHILOSOPHY
Core Beliefs, Loosely Held, Loudly Practiced

Arrive Early
A practical choice disguised as superstition. Being early fixes problems you don't know you'll have yet.

Blue Cheese
Not a preference. A baseline assumption. Visible chunks indicate honesty.

Char
Flavor earned through adversity. Burn is something else entirely.

Cold
A condition acknowledged briefly, then ignored.

Confidence
Required for grilling, parking, and speaking about matchups. Often misplaced. Still necessary.

Consistency
Doing the same unreasonable thing at the same time every week until it starts making sense.

Duct Tape
Structural solution. Emotional support. Universal answer.

Extra Table
An admission that something will fail and that you planned for it.

Foil Pan
Infrastructure. Not disposable until proven useless.

Grill Face
The expression you make when the flame misbehaves and you pretend this was the plan.

Hand Warmers
Tiny miracles. Always gone when you need them most.

"It's Fine"
A lie told with good intentions.

Layers
The difference between enduring and enjoying.

Mayor
The person who knows everyone and everything and never sits down.

Napkins
A finite resource treated as infinite until it isn't.

Parking Spot
Not a location. A legacy.

Patience
Developed by waiting for food, friends, and better officiating.

Propane
Life force. Checked twice. Trusted once.

Ranch
Permitted only under strict, specific circumstances.

Same Spot
Where the day works the way it's supposed to.

Sauce
Language. Memory. Binding agent.

Silence
Acceptable only right before kickoff.

Snow
Decoration. Occasionally structural.

Thermos
A container that never holds what it claims to.

"We'll Figure It Out"
The entire operating system.

Wind
An opponent that never gets tired.

Wings
Not food. Proof of belonging.

ABOUT THE AUTHOR

Mark Donnelly, known professionally as Dr.Donnelly, has spent a career paying attention to how people actually behave, not how they claim they do on paper.

As a writer, lecturer, and longtime observer of human systems, he's learned that the most important rules are rarely written down. They live in habits, rituals, and the quiet agreements groups make without ever holding a meeting. Parking lots, it turns out, are excellent places to study this.

Dr. Donnelly is the author of several books that explore food, culture, survival, and the logic you only discover when things get a little messy, including 50 Shades of Gravy, Goose the Cook, Survival Juice, Poultry in Motion, and How to Eat a Buffalo–a title that has required clarification in multiple social settings.

Based in Western New York, Donnelly has stood through enough wind, snow, heartbreak, and improbable hope to understand that Buffalo Bills tailgating isn't a pastime. It's a practice. One built on food, faith, repetition, and the shared decision to show up even when conditions suggest otherwise.

This book grew out of those observations. Not from the stands, but from the asphalt. From grills that refuse to retire, folding tables with short life expectancies, and conversations that start with food and end somewhere deeper.

When he's not writing, Mark can usually be found explaining why there is always next year.

 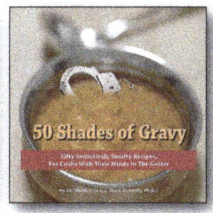    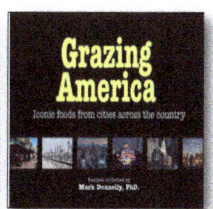

www.ingramcontent.com/pod-product-compliance
Lightning Source LLC
Chambersburg PA
CBHW051550220426
43671CB00024B/2992